# CONTRADICTIONS

## LIYA ENDALE

Published in the United States by

Global Education Foundation Inc.
P.O. Box 83314
Conyers, GA 30013
globaleducationfoundationinc.org

Cover Photo by Caiti Quiza
Book Editors: Crystal Adams and Chris Mays
Formatting by: Liya Endale and Britney LaRoche

Copyright © 2014 Liya Endale
All rights reserved.
ISBN: 0692291849
ISBN-13:978-0-692-29184-9

# DEDICATION

For Ezana and Thrandon

# CONTENTS

**Acknowledgements**
**Introduction** ix

## Nature
A Flickering Flame 4
New Orleans Before the Waters Came 5
Nature's Marvel; A Crow's Convention 6
Perspective 7
A New Day 8
Faith 9
Much in Common 10

## Race
Waiting Shadows 12
Black Angel 13
Black Man 15
Faux Pas 16
Community Service 18

## Ethnicity
I Am Ethiopia 26
Faux Pas II 27
Civil War 29
Reality Check 30
Coming to America 31

## Love
Forgiveness 37
Love 38
Missing Mistaken for Love 39
Broken Hearted Love 40
Eternity 41
Fire Love 42
One Kind of Family 43

**Fun**

| | |
|---|---|
| Just About a Strawberry That Has Gone Bad | 45 |
| Nostalgia | 46 |
| Program Coordinator: What I Do at Work | 48 |
| Can't Sleep | 50 |
| In Denial: A Conversation Between a Rat and an Alien | 52 |
| Contradictions | 55 |

**Self-Empowerment**

| | |
|---|---|
| A Diary Entry | 58 |
| I Am | 59 |
| Forgotten Child | 60 |
| Beast | 62 |
| A Lesson From Fate About Unanswered Questions | 63 |
| Conquering Fear | 65 |
| My Song | 66 |
| We are Eternal | 67 |
| Change | 68 |
| Conquering Demons | 69 |
| Transcending Judgment | 70 |
| Like the Rain in Paris- A Short Story | 71 |

# ACKNOWLEDGMENTS

Mom, Dad and Pebbles, you made me.
Thrandon, you saved me.
Ezana, you are me.
Crystal, you build me up.
Dr. Bailey, Dr. Kleiber, Dr. Moshi, Dr. Ojo and Ms. Shirley, you expect the best of me.
Jerome, Life and Montu, you inspire me.

# INTRODUCTION

That which drives me crazy is the same thing which keeps me sane. For in this life, contradiction is the only constant. We change, evolve, digress, adapt, learn and are always becoming. Contradiction is the human condition. It is time we embrace this truth instead of allowing our denial to keep us from our potentials.

The contradiction of the human mind lies in the fact that we are capable of enormous thoughts but have to think small to interact sanely with each other. I grow weary of small talk. Yet, I miss it when I am burdened with big thoughts. For example, I can't imagine that I will live my entire life not knowing what it is like to be absolutely still. Even in the quietest of places, we are still tethered to this spinning planet, still hurdling through space at speeds we can not comprehend, still constantly fighting gravity with every breath and every heartbeat. Most of us will not, in this life, know silence as we have grown accustomed to the sound of air in our ears – a constant static noise giving us audio reference. Alone, I feel as though I can soar through the cloaked cosmos. Then, I am sucked back to the small things when I interact with others. For this teasing through intentions is necessary to forge meaningful relationships. "No, that's not what I said." "What do you mean?" "Let me clarify." "I must have misunderstood you." "Oh. I see what you mean now."

Though we are all connected we are still each uniquely manifested in this universe. To communicate effectively, we must first understand the uniqueness in each of our perspectives then learn a language that transcends those differences.

Further, we could spend lifetimes exploring our potential and still not comprehend its pinnacle. But here we are none the less, capable of the most divine love between us, fighting through the small talk and pain we inflict upon each other. We unknowingly hope endlessly for those moments when we connect with one another on a deeper level. There, we ride the same wave of energy and experience the elation that comes with this brief journey, if even for a moment. When you are open to it, this elusive type of connection happens spontaneously with people whom you may not expect to share this sacred moment with, in even the most mundane of places. And then, life transcends. The big things manifest in the small things and everything is full of meaning that propels you into your potential. This is my goal. For when I live my life this way, I sleep better at night. I love more purely. I pray more effectively. I fear less. I inspire. I change this place we share into a better world. This transformative journey begins with myself and all of the contradictions that accompany me. I want to be healthy but I skip the gym when I am too tired to get up in the morning. I believe in peace and forgiveness, but I still have my pet-peeves and get angry. I believe in being conscientious but I still stick my foot in my mouth. However, that is how I am made and I strive to forgive myself and everyone else daily instead of launching futile attempts to change the essence of who we are. In order to connect with others and our potentials, inspire others to reach theirs and in order to affect positive and intentional change in this world, we must first stop trying to overcome our contradictions and, instead, embrace them. Our energy is not meant for such misguided efforts. These efforts are small compared to what we are meant to do. Our energy is meant for us to reach higher than we imagine, to connect to a greater purpose and shift its currents with our voices. Inner peace and true confidence ensue. Then, those things we would spin our wheels to attain- love, patience, understanding, success, wisdom- emerge in us as if a by-product. The truth is that they were in us all along. We were too busy trying to be perfect to notice.

## NATURE

*Let us spend much time outside, lest we forget our place in this realm.*

In nature lie clues to our existence. The average person has more questions about her purpose here than she has answers. Because of the nature of the human psyche, this ambiguity about who we really are and where we come from can make it difficult to find purpose for ourselves. But then we can look at a crackling, hypnotizing fire in our fireplace, or perhaps at a bon fire. This energy that is red and yellow and translucent has a purpose here- to burn. Does it have intention? Does it need to understand its purpose? It just is. And it is magnificent. Beautiful and captivating. It can also destroy and cause pain. Whether we encounter it on a cozy winter night or run from it as it chases us from our homes, fire remains stoic. It is our perception of it, based on the context of our interaction, that makes it good or bad. So is it good or bad? Without it, we could not live. Too much will kill us. So, it is both. As are we. Yet, we fight so hard to convince ourselves that we are good people. Then, when we do something "bad," the contradiction of who we think we are versus what we do creates cognitive dissonance. Sometimes, we choose to live in denial or rationalize the "bad" things we do. Other times, we feel defeated and let our self-esteem sink until we become immobilized. What we cannot do is make this contradiction go away. Instead of perceiving ourselves in this moral dichotomy, we can be like fire and accept this contradiction. Within the ensuing peace, we make sound decisions that grow love. When was the last time you saw something in nature that stilled your soul and reminded you to get out of your head?

*Contradictions: Nature*

A Flickering Flame

A flickering flame
At the end of a match
Dances in jubilee
At the miracle of
A single stroke
And for a brief moment
It shines

*Liya Endale*

New Orleans: Before the Waters Came

With stoic anticipation
Somber regard to tragedy
Pain like Pompeii
You met nature
Face to face
In her glory
She raked her teeth
Upon your faith
Now there lives
A distant memory
Before the waters came

*Contradictions: Nature*

## Nature's Marvel; A Crow's Convention

On an average spring day in Georgia, I sat swinging on the back porch. It was the time of year when the weather began to gear-up for the summer days of 'Hot-lanta'. The roof was made of clear, hard plastic, allowing sunlight to filter through and rain to play the type of music which lulls your mind to silence. The air felt especially fresh after a winter which seemed to hush nature. That was when the first three crows appeared. I'd seen these three crows in the mornings all winter, hopping through a grey world on my way to work every morning. They were ride-or-die kind of crows, like a real family. No sooner had they landed than they began to send out a call. It was out of sync at first, but then gained unison like when your turn signals at a light eventually begin to blink in the same rhythm as the car in front of you. Then, they paused. There began to arrive distant calls as though the crows had sent out vocal boomerangs catching airless currents back to their source. But these were not their echoes. They were voices of more crows who eventually found their way to the massive tree which loomed over the house. The new group of five began to synchronize their "Caws" and then stopped as though on cue from a conductor. The calls came back from several directions this time as crows began to glide in from their various boroughs. The ritual repeated three, maybe four times; the calls getting louder each time until the tree was full of crows murmuring occasionally to each other but all concentrating on the task at hand. When the decision was made that all the delegates were in attendance, there was a moment where the simultaneous fluttering of 30-40 wings made me catch my breath. And they were off. My tree, which I realized was never mine at all, was empty again as the crows took off in all directions without so much as a discussion about what was going on. Processing what I had just witnessed, I said to myself quietly, "Did these crows just have a damn convention in my backyard?"

Perspective

Rivers flow through your veins
As small to you as the
Nile is to the universe
Under a stethoscope
You can hear your liquid surge
Your heart is your core
Like the forge whose heat
Churns the stuff of this earth
Sitting in the clouds, you see
Wrinkles on the landscape that look
Like your skin
This planet breathes
Its lungs hidden in the
Green of a leaf
Are we but cells of this organism?
Made of cells
Made of cells?
And I marvel
From core
To core

*Contradictions: Nature*

A New Day

The days fall around me
Like spent coals in a fire
In this comfortable space
I've hewn for myself
I settle into monotony and predictability
Until something jolts me
Always something
That tears apart clouds
And the sun shines blindingly
A new day dawns

## Faith

Like a mole in the Earth
I will blindly seek the light
Like a single flower in the desert
I will bloom in a desolate place
Like a rainbow in the sky
I will shine after the storm
Like the surging river and its calm sea
I will race to my resting place
Like a thirsty camel at an oasis
I will have my thirst quenched
Like the leaping squirrels in the trees
I will not fear a fall
Like the moss by the river
I will cling to my rock
Like the morning dew that disappears
My tears will, too, be dried

*Contradictions: Nature*

Much in Common

I am born of friction
And from that moment
I search for unknown things
My nature propels me
To find a place where I belong
I step out of the clouds
Timid, reaching
Until I find you
Born again
I rip apart the air
And with a thunderous sound
I pour my love into you
My purpose fulfilled
Such a short life
Lived before a blink
That sears Earth

*Liya Endale*

## RACE

Outside of fairy tales of santas & easter bunnies- never has something that does not exist been so real.

When I heard that scientists had mapped our entire genome and had not found the gene that determines race, I was astounded. Race does not exist. It is a completely socially constructed concept that has segregated this planet, started wars and torn hearts apart. There is so much we don't believe in as a society. Aliens and ghosts are concepts that don't really have a place in our legal, educational or punitive systems. If your house gets robbed by an alien that then flies off into space, there is really no way of pressing charges. I doubt your insurance will cover your losses. However, the state of Alabama just repealed a law that forbids inter-racial marriage not long ago. And so, the contradiction of human nature once again has given me a land-mine to navigate. Before this revelation, we had something concrete to explain away all of the confounding choices we have made throughout history. When that was taken away, I had to learn to accept the fact that we had been guided by a fairy-tale.

The intricacy of the collective human mind is incredible. That which we believe to be true can be indistinguishable from that which is true. Once I accepted this, the world made so much more sense.

## Waiting Shadows

I carry this brown sticky
Dense like the atmosphere
Sitting on our heads
Clinging to me
Like a noon-time shadow
Stroke its supple plump
Hide ashy corners bearing
Caramel-chocolate, honey-almond
Carry it- natural as spring time
Haunting like a shadow
Heavy like air on shoulders
Until I shed its weight and
Rise up
Up into the stratosphere
With no oxygen weighing me down
I float in cold
So cold it's hot
So hot it melts
My brown sticky oozing
Over stooped shoulders
Dripping

        Down

                Down

To where my shadow waits

Black Angel

Sitting on the edge of the old porch, she ran the water from the hose over her feet, which changed from a light sandy color to a dark mahogany, glistening in the hot sun. First, she wiped the sweat from her forehead, each drop a tenuous facsimile of the reprieve the hose would bring from the maddening heat. She knew that if she gave into this temptation and got her hair wet, it would translate into hours of work to fix it back up that night. After only a moment's hesitation, Danny leaned her head back. Bringing the hose up above her, she let the cold fingers run rivers through her thick strands, over her face and down the front of her sweat stained tank-top. The cold shocked her body and made her catch her breath, allowing some water in her mouth. She drank it gratefully.

"Danny! What the hell you think you're doin? Who d'ya reckon's gonna have to fix your hair tonight?" Mama ran a tight ship. She didn't have much time for foolishness maintaining this old country house on her own. The kids were actually her daughter's, but they grew up with her their whole lives so they knew her as Mama. She saved Wednesday and Sunday evenings for washing, parting, greasing and braiding Danny's long course hair. Today was Friday.

"I couldn't help it, Mama. It's just so blazin' hot and the boys get to play in the water all the time," she whined.

"The boys don't look like wild children when they're done, either. Cuz they aint got no hair."

None of that stuff mattered to Danny. All she wanted to do was enjoy some sanctuary from the scorching Georgia heat. She stamped into the house, slammed the door so hard some more of the old green paint chipped off, and waited.

"Dammit, girl! You're gonna stop slammin' my door!"

With a satisfied grin, she headed for her small room in the back of the house, resolved not to do anything if she couldn't do something fun.

Sitting in front of an old foggy mirror with chipping edges, she began examining herself closely. By now her hair had risen up all around her head, transforming into a thick, jet black cloud of which her face was the center. It was so heavy it pushed down past her forehead as if perched on her long lashes. She had to admit, she couldn't recall any proper folks she'd seen with hair like that. Women who had hair like this were on the news, protesting and getting arrested. Danny quickly pulled all of the hair back into a fuzzy pony- tail, using gel to slick down the sides. She stared at herself again, observing the marked transformation from what Mama called a wild- child to a semi-presentable young girl. She continued to watch as the short hairs around her face vehemently defied the straightening goop and began curling in towards her forehead, one at a time until she had a lucid mane like a baby lion. It reminded her of the pictures in Mama's old bible that she got from an African lady at church once. All the angels had brown skin and a fuzzy light around their heads instead of halos.

"See, Mama. I don't look like a wild-child." Danny said aloud to herself. "I look like an angel."

*Liya Endale*

Black Man

    Today I was jolted from my every-day, any-day, day-to-day by the milky fog perched outside of my second story window. Surrendering to its beckoning I rose, leaning into the haze. It wanted me only to see the figure below walking across the field, holding a small box, shoulders arched slightly forward with wisdom, strides patient and deliberate, crown dusted with grey, skin browned with ancient roots. It was you, Black Man. Though you were two stories away I could see your kango hat and dark scarf draped over your pea-coat. Though you were two stories away I saw the depth of your eyes a hundred thousand stories deep and in that moment I wanted more than anything to hear each one of these stories. What have they seen that has taught you to walk with such humble dignity? What is it you carry in front of you that commands both of your hands? Where is this object's place and is it grateful that you carry it there so delicately? What burdens hunch your shoulders so, other than this cloud that has chosen them as its perch? What is it you need today? Can I offer you my appreciation?
    The hardest thing I did today was to fight the urge to fly down the stairs, burst open the barrier between me and a lost bit of sky and find you. I want to know your name for now, just to inform you that your energy disrupted my day in the purest way. You may not be an honest man or sweet like your eyes turned down at the corners. But I have not come to judge you. Just to admire your stride and respect your path. I want to thank you for inspiring me more than anything today, Black Man.

Contradictions: Race

Faux Pas

Though I enjoy being social, at times, I enjoy solitude as much. I have no problem going to the park or even to a movie by myself. Alone, I am not distracted from observing the things in life that should be noticed more often. I don't tote around an ipod or send faxes through my super-computer cell phone (In fact, I don't even have a camera on my phone.) This one time in particular, I was sitting in an eatery enjoying a Philly Cheese Steak like it was 1990 again (technologically speaking, anyway). I even left my phone in my car.

Pretending my meaty hoagie was actually cool enough to eat, I would attempt a bite, followed by a pause, and attempt a bite again. Hunger makes us repeat those unproductive cycles, futile attempt after futile attempt at satiating that carnal need to feed... reducing us to the barbaric, unreasoning beings we supposedly evolved from. I can't explain it, just the way it is sometimes.

I was disturbed from my zombie-like state by a man who hobbled in the door on crutches. Even though he had a companion to help him he still made quite a clatter, crashing his metal poles on the doorway. Everyone looked up. He came in even more conspicuously, waving and nodding to all three groups of us patrons enjoying our good 'ole American food. I was close enough to hear him say to his companion, "Oh, Chinese! I love Chinese!"

Bewildered I put my sandwich down and turned to look towards the counter. The lady working that day was, indeed, Asian. But I would have guessed Vietnamese. I shook my head and was trying to give the man the benefit of the doubt. Maybe he was just continuing a conversation with his companion about what they should order for the Sunday night get-together coming up. It was All-Star weekend, after all.

The hobbling man seemed to hear my thoughts and decided to stick the nail in the coffin. He went to the counter and said, "Hi. Let me get some shrimp fried rice."

I turned to look at the door he just theatrically entered through. On the backdrop of a huge American Flag was written the name of the establishment: "American Deli."

"I'm sorry, sir. We don't serve Shrimp Fried Rice here."

*Contradictions: Race*

Community Service

It was Saturday morning and time to wake up at 7 am once again. Though accustomed to these early morning hours with my full- time job at the University of Georgia, Saturday is the only morning of the week when I wake up excited for the coming day. I volunteer with local high-school students in the community, helping give them part of an academic advantage they deserve but might not get elsewhere. I realize my enthusiasm is fueled by the fact that I am the rookie of a team of Masters students already in the School Counseling Program, a program to which I have just been accepted. I look for every opportunity to feed this hunger I have to do big things; specifically to make a difference in the lives of these sassy high-schoolers.

This Saturday would be different. One of the program directors had an idea to hold a mock trial for the seniors as some of their grades had been slipping of late. She had a theory that the slipping grades were more an indication of latent fears the students were experiencing as opposed to senior-itis, procrastination or a lack of understanding of the materials. The seniors were going to be put on trial for various fears they had been experiencing; such as fear of leaving home, success, expectations of others or themselves and hard work. Equipped with a judge, bailiff, prosecuting and defense attorneys, and a jury, the trial began. I sat in the back row of the jury and observed the scene. The director began with an assertion and conviction in her tone which instantaneously melted any skepticism that this trial was, indeed, a serious matter. I involuntarily straightened up in my chair and observed the other students in the classroom doing the same. Our first senior was called to the stand and sworn in.

"Do you swear to tell the truth, the whole truth, and nothing but the truth so help you Dr. Bailey?" The bailiff asked. Dr. Bailey was a founder of the program. With a tickled smile, the student on trial obliged. He was failing every one of his classes at the mid-way point of his final semester. Our director, the Prosecuting Attorney, had him read his grades to the courtroom. After the shocked murmurs and "tisk tisks" from the courtroom and a quick "Order in the court!" from the judge, his defense attorney, a math tutor in the program, attempted to give him an out.

"With a part-time job, responsibilities at home and social obligations, can you tell the courtroom how someone can expect you to devote even more time to your studies?"

With the type of innocence reserved for only the purest hearts, the student retorted by honestly saying, "Well, I don't *have* to play so many video games or go out so much with my friends." I smiled as his innocence and honesty humbled me.

The next senior to the stand admitted he only used 30% of his potential. This 30% got him into two of the five colleges he applied to. The math tutor pointed out that these accomplishments deemed this student a success. Next, a junior was called to the stand. The director brought up an instance when this student had waited until the last moment to ask for help with a paper, emphasizing that the volunteers in the program can only help students if they come to us in time.

The time came for the jury to deliberate. I led them into the hallway where we began with an initial vote on whether or not the students in the case of Empowered Youth Programs (EYP) versus the students of EYP were, in fact, guilty of the charged crime; fear. I was surprised that only one student and myself stood on the 'guilty' side of the hallway. I wanted to hear the possible justification of a 'not-guilty' verdict after such a compelling case from the prosecution.

"Well," began the first of the 'not-guilty' voting jury, "I don't think the students are guilty because they are trying to make good grades. I could see if they just weren't trying at all."

The next person in that group continued, "The math teacher had a point that his client got into two of the five colleges he applied to and the other student who was failing all his classes got into a school, too. Isn't that the point of the program?"

I took a moment to take in what the students were saying and structure my counter argument. The intimidating 'not-guilty' voters

## Contradictions: Race

tried to coerce my sole 'guilty' voting companion to their side and I saw her struggling with a decision.

"What do *you* think?" I asked her. "Remember, I'm asking for your honest opinion regardless of what anyone else thinks, including me."

"Well, I think they're guilty because their grades are not good and I think they could have done a lot better."

I admired her courage to think for herself and her ability to evaluate the situation beyond the surface. For the second time that day, I smiled at the humility the students made me feel.

"I agree," I began. "Each senior admitted that he was not using more than 30% of his potential. That's not fair to the program and that's not fair to themselves. The directors worked very hard to put over a million dollars into this program and I don't think 30% potential is a fair tradeoff."

The 'not-guilty' jury voters began to look down at their shoes as though they were guilty themselves. They mumbled their assent and moved to the other side of the hallway. One 'not-guilty' voter was left, a volunteer in the program. His resolved demeanor made me believe we would be in the hallway for quite some time. We all looked at him expectantly and he began his argument, "The students are actually working hard. It's not easy to do so many things at once and I think they do deserve a bit of a break. They all got into college and we shouldn't forget the amount of work they put in to be accepted, especially because they spend so much more time outside of EYP in a world that doesn't believe they can succeed. We should take that into account and focus on the good rather than focusing on their shortcomings. I think they're not guilty." I saw his cogent remarks begin to stir some ambivalence amongst the group, "The math tutor had a good point during his closing arguments." He continued, "Sometimes the results of our work won't show up until later. Maybe we need to be more patient and give the group some time to show better results."

I knew I had to act fast. "It is true that we should praise the students for getting into some of the schools they got into. However, if they've admitted they're not using even half of their potential and we know that they're smart enough to get into all of their schools, aren't we as guilty of placing the same lower expectations on them as society? Also, how can we expect any results to assess if this program is working if they don't do their best? They have a responsibility here to try their best so we can accurately see if our efforts are working. They are on trial today for fear of other people's expectations who do not think they can be great. This program should not be a part of those expectations and that fear. We all know these students could have gotten into all of the schools they applied to and if we don't hold them accountable, no one else will."

Our one adversary reflected for a moment and I stood in anticipation.

"I guess I was evaluating the situation subjectively. Objectively, though, you are right."

"So, do we have your subjective or objective vote for the jury?" I asked hopefully.

"I vote guilty."

Marching back into the courtroom, the first student who courageously voted guilty read our verdict out loud. We summarized our reasoning to the group which seemed to agree with our decision. The director then began a discussion. Her words, combined with her disarming approach, seemed to put everyone at ease after an intense deliberation. It was a matter of moments before we got to the heart of this fear the students were put on trial for. The students were, in fact, scared. They were scared of leaving home, not because home was a place where they were given things freely, but because some of them were the backbones of their families. Two students shared some very difficult struggles they had after their families endured unimaginable hardships. Fighting back tears, I looked around the room. There were more wet eyes than dry. Students and volunteers alike were touched by the strength and the pain of two high-school students who carried the weight of the world on their shoulders. First, I wondered how many people were crying out of sympathy and how many were crying because the stories hit home since they, too, were dealing with things that they had not shared with anyone. Then, I came to the realization that we had two more courageous warriors amongst us. The fact that they were able to admit that their struggles did, in fact, create fear in their lives instead of trying to put on a façade that nothing bothered them gave their peers permission to do the same.

What impressed me even more was the fact that these two students are two of the students who always come to Saturday Academy with a smile and enough strength to encourage others to work harder. The last statement one of these students made was about the other students who had stopped coming to EYP. It made the hair stand up on the back of my neck.

"They are the ones who failed us."

Personally, I am torn. I know that some of the students in EYP have endured more of life than some of us volunteers. Is it fair to expect more from them than we've ever had to expect from even ourselves? The lone volunteer who held on to a not-guilty vote until the end did make a great point. Not to take into account the life these students face outside of EYP would make our efforts impractical. At the same time, I know that my responsibility as a counselor and as someone who wants to make a difference means that I have to put sympathy aside. Sympathy and guilt, though virtuous characteristics, are two of the most debilitating factors that ensure that many minorities stay in a stagnant state of negative statistics. Empathy is the key to moving forward, as was told to me that day from another student named in the hallway. Pushing these students to fulfill their potential without the same resources as the rest of the country is going to be a much more difficult task than I anticipated. It's always easier to let fear stop you from expecting more of yourself and allow it to make you succumb to the expectations of a world which has stopped believing in you. As a volunteer, it is also easier to succumb to the sympathy we feel as good people and give the students a break instead of continuing to push them when we see life weighing on their shoulders. This program can not exist with the efforts of just one side. This day, I realized that I would need the amazing strength of these students to continue to do my part. They, in turn, deserve our strength to fight the ideas this world has of them.

Years later, I continue to hear one of the student's words ringing in my ears. The students and volunteers of EYP need each other as it is only a concerted effort which can lead to positive results. I now understand what she meant when she said of the other students who do not come every Saturday, "They are the ones who failed us."

*Liya Endale*

## ETHNICITY

Laced into our DNA, we carry the legacy of our ancestors.

Our DNA tells millions of stories: stories of love and hate, war and triumph, hope and despair. We are made of the stories of people who many believe have walked this planet for over two million years. Though we do not know all of their names or every place that they have lived, their lives are locked into those smallest pieces of us. Though we do not know what scars they carried, we know they survived the most trying times. How many times did one of your ancestors almost lose his or her life before they bore the progeny responsible for your existence? How many times were you almost not born? Somehow, a series of unlikely events have led me to sit in front of my computer and share my story with you. Though I live a very American life, I am still the culmination of Ethiopian history. And though I feel like a bit of a stranger in my birth land, I am grateful for it and pay respect to every mother and father who came before me.

*Contradictions: Ethnicity*

I Am Ethiopia

I understand that
Look of your eyes
The nod of your head
The suck of your breath
As you say yes
The wrinkles in your lips
The curl of your hair
The angle of your neck
As you greet the world
Your essence is that of
Milk and honey
Rugged elegance
Enduring splinters of
Untamed wood
Your hands tell stories
That piece together
Mankind's telling
And untelling
Your trenches
Contain secrets that
Would unravel
Our feeble minds
From your womb
Was birthed the best
And worst of
Humankind
Let your horn sound
For the world to hear
The music of our history

*Liya Endale*

Faux Pas II

I love religion. I love the customs and traditions that vary so widely. Some sing and dance, some teach of somber and disciplined ways, some chant and meditate, and some speak in another language even they don't understand. It is a luxurious privilege that I observe these traditions with the f reedom nested in the safe cushion of my right to participate in none or all of them.

Going back home to Ethiopia I realize this luxury translates into social humiliation because religion and culture know no division in some places. As a citizen of this country, it is assumed that you know the basic practices of Islam and Christianity simply because these two religions make up the culture. Even if you go to "Burger Queen" you may be asked if you are fasting that day to determine which menu you receive. If you have a large gathering you know to have a Muslim and a Christian prepare food differently for the guests, if not you might as well put a curse on them.

We were visiting the 8th wonder of the world, Lalibela- this place that has a series of 11 churches, centuries old, hewn into the ground made of hard volcanic rock. It took twenty years to carve these churches that are connected through an intricate series of underground tunnels- in the 12th century. Amazing.

I was slowly making my way in and out of these immaculate churches, following our guide in my oversized Tommy Hilfiger sweatshirt and baggy pants, desperately trying to keep up with his 90 word-a-minute Amharic about the history, the architecture, the legend, the miracle of this place that is still inhabited by practicing Christian Orthodox priests. Still trying to make sense of the big words rattling in my brain, I accidentally found myself in some sort of blessing line before a Priest wearing a long, intricately detailed robe and carrying the famous Lalibela cross... a metal, sometimes wooden, cross so elaborately designed with symbolic details that the final product (commonly made into earrings and necklaces) is easily mistaken for a snowflake in the U.S. I didn't have time to think when my sister and I were standing face to face with the holy man himself. I still don't know what happened or what was supposed to

*Contradictions: Ethnicity*

happen. All I know is that I was prayed over, got smacked in the face a couple of times with his cross and likely did something very horrible by doing nothing at all. I stood there utterly confused, blinking profusely and flinching only at the swat of holy metal to my forehead- left to ponder the meaning of my blessed encounter with an Orthodox Priest.

*Liya Endale*

Civil War

Separated by our connection
Divided by common ground
Enmity no longer needs to be understood
Now accepted the way love once was
From opposite sides of the border
We mirror each other's DNA
Still found soaking the Earth
Almond eyes traced in black
Hiding beneath the shadow of
A cliff-like brow
Stripped naked and without words
We do not know our enemy
Let us sit in silence
For peace to dare return
Isn't it beautiful when joy transcends?
Like praise from broken hearts to
Silenced lips
Like music to the Heavens

Reality Check

I climbed a mountain with a boy from this village in Ethiopia where my mother was born. He worked and lived on my grandparents' farm. I assumed he didn't have a family, but as we ascended this massive bulge of earth, I learned that he did, in fact, have a mother, a father and even little brothers and sisters. At the pinnacle, I caught my breath and I asked,
"Where do they live?"
He pointed to the horizon and we counted four mountain peaks away. As his finger aligned our gaze, he said, "There."
Hazy from the bits of cloud that hovered between us, his home looked so far away. I imagined being 16 and living that far from my family with no phone to call or car to visit.
"How did you get here?"
He smiled and I knew I'd asked a silly question.
"I walked."
I thought about how long it had taken me to climb this mountain and how tired I was and how long it would take me to climb back down, and up, and down, and up, and down, and up, and down and up.
"Why?"
"Of course," he answered. "To go to school."

Coming to America

We didn't come to the United States until I was seven years old. At the first sight of Dallas, Texas from my airplane window, I thought the stars had fallen out of the sky and landed in a puddle of twinkling lights.

"Daddy, is that where we will live?" I whispered to my father in Dutch.

"It is. Do you like it?"

"It looks like a dream." I replied, never taking my eyes away from the window.

A representative from our sponsoring Catholic Church gave us a ride to our first apartment on US soil. There would be no living with others in this democratic land where privacy is revered. I was too little to see out of the window of the big American car, but we finally arrived. We set our bags down in our new home. The small government housing projects sat on the north side of the city. A single yellow light bulb gave the place an eerie feel and the air smelled like old carpet, cleaning supplies and wet clothes. Luckily for us, there was only one bed because we were not able to pack enough sheets and comforters for four. My mother began to open suitcases right away. First, she draped covers over the bed in the only bedroom, folding the sheet back over the comforter like in a fancy hotel, even though we were going to go to sleep very soon. The beige, floral pattern instantly gave us a familiar reference to ease our nerves. My father slept on the floor beside us as my sister and I squeezed in next to my mother on the mattress. No one knew what the next day would bring and there was little conversation.

Life became a blank canvas on which I began to imagine my next adventure. I saw myself riding horses on a farm like the characters in the soap opera, *Dallas*. Soon, I would be swimming in our pool nestled behind our massive farm-house in the middle of endless stretches of bright green grass. I wondered if I would meet JR, my favorite character from the show. Too excited to sleep, I shifted from side to side beneath the stifling covers and listened to my mother breathing lightly beside me. She never moved in her sleep, not even a finger. Her face did not contort into gruesome expressions like mine with the threat of drool glistening at the corners of her mouth. Instead, she would lie still as a porcelain doll dipped in caramel. I would study each of her delicate features that appeared painted on her face with an artist's brush; her eyes lined with feathery lashes, her nose arched perfectly down the center of her face, her regal cheekbones proudly giving off an air of elegance, and her lips the color of a pink rose cast in an afternoon shadow. Even I was not too young to know that she was a rare beauty and resolved that growing up to contain half of that beauty would be enough for me. More would be overwhelming, like she was at first sight.

I wondered if the moonlight peeking in through the window blinds came from the same moon which appeared back home in Holland. I quickly decided it must have been a different moon. How would it have traveled all of those hours across the ocean so quickly to make it to the Netherlands that same night? Eventually, my endless wonderment faded into the dream realm.

The morning sun shed new light on our new world. I cracked open the plastic blinds over the window in the living-room and scanned the landscape. Even first light carried an intense heat that made the air seem to waver like a mirage in a desert. I marveled at the small yard with patchy grass and the weathered fence which created a permeable border between the row of square lawns and the rest of my new world. I looked for potential friends but it seemed that this new world was slow to rise. "Daddy, where are the other children?" I asked, this time in our native tongue, Amharic. It did not seem appropriate to speak Dutch in a new country.

"I do not know, honey. Maybe they are still sleeping."

"Emwedish? Where are the other kids to play with?" This time I asked my mother, calling her by her house name meaning 'the one whom I adore.'

"They are eating their breakfast so they can hurry and play with you today. They're excited to meet you."

My eyes widened with excitement.

"They know we're here already? Who told them?"

"Everyone knows we're coming, dear. Watch how quickly you make new friends."

My sister and I looked on from the weathered breakfast table as my parents found the box of Rice Krispies and the milk that was left for us by our friends from the Catholic Church. My father poured the flakes into a small wooden bowl, added a bit of milk which came in a strange plastic carton and mixed it with a spoon from the drawer. He slowly tasted it, thoughtfully, before he gave it to my sister and me.

"What is it?" My sister asked as her face scrunched up.

"It's breakfast. Now eat it." My farther retorted dryly.

She looked at me and tasted the strange concoction that sounded like tiny little fireworks. She sputtered and coughed but managed to swallow the first bite.

"This milk tastes rotten!" She exclaimed.

"It's not rotten. It's just different in America. You'll get used to it."

And so we learned to get used to mass produced bread instead of the fresh baked loaves from the market, orange and purple drinks that tasted like liquid sugar instead of the orange juice we squeezed every morning, waxy icing on birthday cake instead of the creamy, fluffy stuff that tasted like sweet air and plastic cheese singles instead of the kind that came in wedges that we sliced for each sandwich.

We had to learn about hop-scotch, Cabbage Patch dolls, and Doctor Pepper all at once. It was amazing that something made of peppers could taste so sweet. Truly, only a doctor could accomplish such a feat. People babbled to me in a strange language I recognized from all of those phone calls back in Holland. A fellow Ethiopian girl in my first-grade class who was born in the States would try and explain to everyone why I was so strange.

"She's from another place far away. They don't talk English there." She offered this explanation to the kids who crowded around us.

"Hello?" I attempted the only English word I remembered from when my parents picked up a ringing telephone.

Blank eyes stared.

"Talk something in Ethiopian!" Demanded one of the kids who I'd soon learn was the class bully.

Mahader looked at me and shrugged her shoulders. She informed me they wanted to hear Amharic. My eyes lit up as I looked around at them and asked, "Amarenya t'chilalachu inde?!"

They erupted in a burst of giddy laughter.

"Amama tachalalala!!" The boy's derisive babbling shot a pain of embarrassment through me as I looked desperately over at Mahader. Abashedly avoiding my eyes, she answered my question by telling me the kids did not, in fact, speak Amharic but only wanted to hear it.

I slowly began my integration into American culture, learning that staying quiet and observing everything was a key element in preserving much chagrin. With great patience, I confronted ridiculous questions by repeatedly professing that we did have cars in Africa, we did not eat other people in Africa, and our house was made of full brick and not straw and sticks. Quickly, I learned that when people called me shy, they were not actually telling me they wanted a cup of *shai*, or tea. Once, the teacher told two students to stop fussing, and I exploded in a fit of laughter which caught the attention of the class. Mahader looked at me and slowly caught on to what had caused my histrionic fit. She giggled politely with one hand over her mouth and explained to the class that *fuss* actually meant *fart* in Amharic. As the class burst into laughter again, she explained to me that fuss did not have any gas-passing connotation in English.

Assimilating to a new culture inevitably involves moments of severe regret and a complete re-assessment of one's ego. Luckily, I came here at an age when learning languages was more of a game, a phonetic puzzle that did not differ from learning Amharic or Dutch in the Netherlands. I became fascinated with the English language and its counter-intuitive idiosyncrasies. By the next year, I offered the word "xylophone" when asked to come up with a word that began with X during an oral assessment in the first-grade. My teacher's mouth fell open as the wrong words took turns forming on her lips. I knew I had done something right and couldn't wait to go home and tell my parents so as to bring them honor.

*Contradictions: Love*

# LOVE

We are each a unique manifestation of the universe capable of the most divine love.

Is there anything more wrought with contradiction than love? It is those whom we love the most capable of hurting us the most. Yet, we still hurtle into this terrifying place with one another. Why? Because love is inevitable. It is a part of the fabric of our nature. It is not love that hurts and confuses us. It is actually our flaws as humans that adulterate love as soon as it is filtered through our complicated hearts. But even with the muddled mess that we make of it, its beauty shines. And with time and diligence, humility and patience - we can experience the most divine love. That is when we, as a people, are at our best.

Forgiveness

And when they do not understand
Forgive them without apology
Those who love you most

*Contradictions: Love*

Love

Love weighs
As gravity tugs at its edges
Mass like a teaspoon full of
A dying star
Dense with ambiguity
Potential of a black hole

*Liya Endale*

Missing, Mistaken for Love

I am tormented by
Missing you
I roll this terrible pleasure
Around in my mouth
Tongue-ing its
Grooves and crevices
So bitter-sweet
I can't get enough

*Contradictions: Love*

Broken Hearted Love

I hate you because
I love you
Your eyes hold
That space between
My heart beats
Broken to pieces then
Glued together
Precarious as a toddler's
First step
Line me up with your
Double edged sword
While your capricious words,
Arbitrary as tyranny,
Make my head dance in circles
Exchanging sacrifices
A bandy of hollow promises
Your sweet touch
Sour as acid in rain
Not this again
Not this again
Make me forget
Make me
Me Again

*Liya Endale*

Eternity

There is

                                                   eternity

                                                                              in        the

silence

                                                                                               between

           your

                    words.

*Contradictions: Love*

Fire Love

Lap at me
Your warmth a
Raging beast
Breath crackling
Soothing sounds
Your roar
Freezes blood
Waiting to be unleashed upon
My lush fields
To devour each blade
But leave behind
Rich soil
To grow stronger

*Liya Endale*

One Kind of Family

At first your glance did make me blush
And then I took your hand
We walked an aisle, made a vow
And then our life began

Two people in a home alone
The wedding music gone
And life resumed for all our guests
We now must build our home

With just a hammer and a nail
We quickly got to work
You in my way and I in yours
We loved as much as hurt

But slowly we did find our beat
And then came our first son
Now a father and a mom
Our hearts are truly won

Your glance at first did make me blush
Then I forgot to look
Now over the head of our sleeping child
Your glance, my breath it took

## FUN

Laughter is the mortar that fills the cracks in our spirit.

We do not yet completely understand how we operate as humans. However, ancient wisdom and modern science indicate that when stress builds up inside of us, it eventually comes out one way or another. Tears are one of these ways; Laughter is another. So cry. But when you can, make them tears of joy.

*Liya Endale*

Just About a Strawberry That has Gone Bad

When first mine eyes do set on thee
How boldly doth thou boast thine seed
Each displayed upon thine breast
Beckoning my need to feed

How brightly doth thine crimson call
That drops of blood before you bow
You put to shame sweet sun-set's hues
Adieu for now, Adieu for now

Yet ho, 'tis this a withered ware?
Withered away before my stare?
How quickly doth thou shrink beneath
Thine strength, thine vice, too much to bear

How quickly doth thou change thine ways
Thine nectar hints of somber grey
When not more than a moment past
It seemed to pass from Zeus's tray

Such beauty that you once contained
Too much at once would cause much pain
Too much for simple minds as ours
Must pass as quickly as it's gained

*Contradictions: Fun*

Nostalgia

I remember when I played so hard
Sweat would roll in beads
From my forehead and cheeks
Collect in a trembling pool
At the tip of my chin
And break free
Back then laughter was free
Outside was heaven
Water hoses spouted
Hopes and dreams
We crawled in
Climbed on
Jumped off
Everything
We sold lemonade for a quarter
Washed cars for five bucks
Then split it 5 ways
We screamed with delight
If we were found hiding
Crouched in dark cabinets
For 15 minutes, forever
Daylight savings was
Like Christmas
A whole HOUR longer
Before the sun went down
And we trailed dirt on the carpet
Angered parents with grass stains
Browned fingernails
And sandy rooted braids
Flushed faces in a
Texas summer
Scared mother of sun stroke warnings
Showing off new scabs and bruises
That never taught us to

*Liya Endale*

Ride slower on curves
Broken bones like war wounds
Busted lips, tales of courage
Fighting back tears 'till we got home
To mother's lap, who never told a sole
We ran as fast
Pedaled as hard
Imagined as far
As we could
We dared life every second
Poked leathery snake eggs with sticks
Caught frogs and toads
Pulled worms apart
We were Kool-Aid sticky
Berry Blast red lipped
Pickle breathed
Bucktooth smiling kids
Wreaking havoc on order
Planted flower beds all in a row
Didn't stand a chance
This was our world

*Contradictions: Fun*

Program Coordinator I – What I do at work

1 "Where is my pencil?"
2 Stapling
3 Copying
4 Getting frustrated because I still can't find my pencil
5 Texting my sister about the pathetic soul that stole my pencil.
6 Minimizing and maximizing the wrong tabs because it takes 50 documents on a single screen to organize one event
7 Sending emails
8 Resending emails that people don't read
9 Looking up sent emails to verify that I did, in fact, send the email that people didn't read
10 Running to the main floor where pencils are kept only to find the original pencil in my hair
11. Apologizing to the pathetic soul I accused of stealing my pencil
12 Deleting emails from reputable bank managers from Hong Kong and Nigeria, agents of Saudi billionaires, and childless widowers of Tsunami relief volunteers calling me "Dear sister in Christ" and "Dear beloved follower of Jesus"
13 Contemplating my dormant potential
14 Sending 800 copies in 67 separate documents to an old printer in the basement which is turned off
15 Texting my sister about the old printer in the basement that Moses used to distribute the 10 commandments
16 Planning my retirement
17 Recycling
18 Figuring out why there are 61 applications on the website but the excel chart only counts 60
19 Adding one more thing to my plate
20 Observing my eye twitch when the old printer in the basement remembers to print my 800 copies in 67 separate documents... two weeks later.
21 Attending Excel workshops to figure out why there are 61 applications on the website and 60 on the Excel chart

22 Learning how to use the paintbrush tool in Microsoft Office documents, how to change margins of footers, how to use Zoomerang survey applications and how to create PDFs from multiple files

23 Feeling accomplished that I now know how to use the paintbrush tool in Microsoft Office, how to change margins of footers, how to use Zoomerang survey applications, and how to create PDFs from multiple files

24 Running to the main office to use the only color printer & pulling the legal paper cartridge slightly out so the printer prints from the cartridge with the regular paper

25 Running back to my office to hit print

26 Running to the main office to clear the paper jam to follow

27 Running back to my office to hit print again

28 Repeat the last two items on this list several times

29 Marveling with teary eyes at the splendid programs delivered from central duplication

30 Dying slightly each time a coworker points out the typo on page eight

31 Reminding visitors to close the door on their way out

32 Doing a dance at 5:00

Contradictions: Fun

Can't Sleep

Tap dancing on the surface of your cerebellum
A little devil dances
Creeps in and out of the folds of your grey matter
Weaving through forgotten memories and
Conjuring up ghosts you thought would lay forever
Squeezing the last drip-drop of life from
Bygones of past eons
Lowering inhibitions about conspiracy theories that
Wouldn't make sense under the mid-day sun
Maybe we didn't land on the moon after-all
Words begin to rhyme themselves into oblivion
Taking rational with them and off they go
Like a storm in the Caribbean
You start planning for the future and realize
The future sometimes plans itself
so why do all the planning
If the plan's been planned? I can't understand
If my clutch is disengaging the gears in the engine
What's engaging the gears in my head?
I have to find my clutch
My crutch like Brick
Like a Cat on a Hot Tin Roof
Dance little devil!
Dance your sick tap tap- sliiiide- heel toe –
Oh no
Just the thought of tomorrow burdens you
Because of your flip-flopped inner time clock
That's not keeping time at all
But the tick tick tick keeps rhythm
For the devil's shoes that click click click
In tune with the meaty guts of your mind
Completely out of sync with man's concept of time
Time and being
Because the mundane going ons that

*Liya Endale*

Begin with the wake and bake of the sun –
Those light, stepping on the surface- learned from repetition drills
We execute
Put my mind to sleep
But boy when that devil gets to tapping
It's like a catalyst to get the neurons firing
In directions they've dreamed about all day in their sleep.

## Contradictions: Fun

In Denial: A conversation between a rat which thinks it's a mouse
and an alien which thinks it's a human

I knew a mouse
A dainty mouse
Which really was a rat

It knew it not
And so it thought
It was a mouse grown fat

"Oh, Mouse," I'd say
"You seem to be
Mistaken don't you see?

Your ears are much
Too small and your
Tail can reach my knee!"

"Oh, really?"
Said this rat to me
Quite- sarcastically

"And what is it
You call yourself?
Human's epitome?

I pray tis not,
My "human" friend,
But just in case tis so

You have a few
More inches that
I'm thinking you must grow

*Liya Endale*

That thing you call
A four-head seems
To carry more like five

Of whatever that it is
you 'humans'
proudly hoard inside."

Shocked, I said,
"Look here, you rat,
I only want to help!

You see even
Your massive droppings
Dwarf that mousy whelp."

"You seem to be,"
He barked at me
"Here from outer space.

Your lanky arms
Mismatch the giant
Eyes there on your face."

"Assuredly
I say to you
I'm quite the human-being.

I'll even prick
Myself to show my
Blood flows red- not green!"

"If you insist,
My 'human' friend
I will agree to that.

*Contradictions: Fun*

You are a human
Just as much as
I am but a rat!"

*Liya Endale*

Contradictions

Flying frogs with silver wings
Ballerinas in the trees
Monkeys swimming in the ocean
And purple shrubs that grow up high
Little hamsters in the forest
Fluffy gators on the sand
Pink specked rain-drops dripping on the
Roof of chocolate candy yams
Curly hair and sugar freckles
Cinnamon shoes with gooey lace
Apple caramel pockets filled
And a smile on every face

## SELF EMPOWERMENT
Can we truly be brave without first knowing fear?

Fear is one of the most powerful human emotions. It is unpleasant and can keep us from our potentials. However, it can also help us reach our pinnacle. The difference is how we use the power that comes from it. You can choose to be courageous. Fear it. Then, lean into it. Every person who we admire has accomplished something that a lot of people would be scared to do. Now, I'm not talking about drag racing on the highway. I'm talking about taking chances on reaching your dreams. I tell my students all the time, we live in a country where you don't ever fail until you stop trying. This does not mean that your path will be fair or easy, just that you can succeed. The choice, however, is yours. Do you want to stay where you are and never know what you are capable of? Or do you want to be extraordinary?

*Contradictions: Self Empowerment*

A Diary Entry

I woke up in a state of woken sleep this morning. I spent eternity connected to the spiritual realm where it is safe. Eventually I forced myself to rise up. Today I am on the bathroom floor. Staring at the contents in the cabinet: shae butter, hydrogen peroxide, pads, first aid kit, shampoo, Q-tips, hair grease, 1 track of Indian weave still in its box. As the mechanical part of me organizes these things, the other part of me, the part which hasn't shaken sleep, consumes me, my spirit, my essence.

I realize I am afraid. I am afraid to engage my gears into this machine which whisks us off to our destinies. I need purpose to reengage. I need a reason greater than my fear.

I Am

I am passion cyclones disrupting edges yearning for peace
I am privileged ignorance interrupted by conviction
I am faith in wounded things worth fighting for
I am picking up forgotten dreams
I am limitless like light and love
I am tempted, learning balance between spontaneity and discipline
I am love and hate and everything in between
I am on a journey in the uncharted territory of my nooks and crannies
I am liquid soul seeping out of my hip-hop
I am Common, Goodie Mob, Mos Def and Black Thought
I am the genesis of mankind
I am stirring contemplation that won't let me rest
I am waiting on permission from no one to unchain this world
To realize that all wrongs in this world
I am too disturbed to be okay with this world
To water down the truth to bite-sized grains for this world

Forgotten Child

I am the forgotten child
Who sits in the back of the class
Doodling alternate worlds in her notebook
Befriending her own thoughts

I am the forgotten child
Who learns to be invisible
Finding comfort in the peripheral
Accepting her forgotten fate

I am the forgotten child
Who singes her hair with hot combs
Damaging perfection for straightened identity
Not realizing how beautiful it is kinky

I am the forgotten child
Who walks alone in this place
Singing songs aloud to ward off silence
Neglecting the liquid soul in her voice

Run, Child, Run!
I cheer myself on
Forgotten by the coaches
They've more important children to coach

I beat my own record
Two minutes
Three minutes faster!
"My grandma runs faster!" Coach yells

Next year I will make Varsity
I will wear that blue plastic leather
And then someone might think
I may be worth remembering

Liya Endale

Next year I run faster
I pass a boy in the race
In front of my coach who looks at him
"Don't worry, you'll catch her!"

I let him catch me
I'm not supposed to be in front
At the banquet I'll get my jacket
I'll just wait for the banquet

Nine girls stand in front
Everyone is clapping
But no one remembers
There are supposed to be 10

I am the forgotten child
Ugly black
Caramel mahogany
Poisoned by ignorance

I am the forgotten child
Afro kinky
Beautiful queen
Isolated in their sins

I am the forgotten child
Awkward weird
Open love
Forced into independence

I am the forgotten child
Cursed with the sweet memory
Of all those who forgot her
And, today, make her amazing

## Contradictions: Self Empowerment

Beast

I'm taught not to pity people with disabilities
But I am sorry that you're so spiritually
Blind to see
That I'm not really 5'3
At all
I'm a beast stomping this earth
Until it quivers beneath me
I've caused earthquakes that
Your richter scales cannot measure
And I hold this treasure
Inside of me
And I rejoice in my divinity
Until you come by
You, who sits so high in this world
I have to strain my neck just to look at your face
And I smile my pretty little smile
Woo you with my witty jokes
And sparkling eyes
And let you continue thinking
That I
Am beneath
You
When really
You never entered the room
There is no room for you in my space
Because I fill it up
With my unique intelligence
Creativity and elegance
And you are surrounded by me
While your air waits outside
Impatiently
For its chance to suffocate
Some poor little person who
Is blind to her own potential

*Liya Endale*

A Lesson from Fate About Unanswered Questions

I get caught in the torrents of it all.
The undertow sweeps me back in right when I think I've landed on the shore.
This tumbling back and forth
At the mercy of fate herself has finally broken my hard shell and I accept that which she has in store.
I can kick, but the strength of my legs will fail before I can match the strength of the ocean.
I can reach for shore
But my reach will prove too short
If fate is not on the same side that I am on.
So I must befriend this omnipresent force,
Charm my way into her favor
Before my frustrations lead me to belabor
Another battle that I have not picked and chosen wisely.
"What is it you know, mighty fate, that I can learn? Do you take us places that are best for us, sweet keeper of souls?"
"I have a job, little one, that you need not concern yourself with."
She replies- and with grand sweeping motions of her arms churns
The deep water and commands its control.
"Oh divine shepherd, I am but a feeble sheep in your flock
And concern is not
A need I have because upon your very shoulders you have carried that burdensome lot.
Forgive me of my ignorance when it comes to the matters that keep you so busy,
But my tenacious curiosity
Will not let me rest. Will you not humor my bothered soul
And tell me one thing that will busy it with thoughts to console?
Then I can leave you to your omnipotent work, humble master."
For a moment so brief I questioned its existence, the waters were As still as a mirror reflecting perfectly the Heavens above.
In that moment, time did not exist.
"Little one," she began, "Though we appear separated we are,

## Contradictions: Self Empowerment

In fact, one- connected in those places we can not yet see.
Just as I have a job you rely upon, so do you have a purpose that
Without- I could not be.
Your purpose is to believe in yourself and since we are one that
Means you believe in me.
Your path is written and that is the only path you will tread.
At the same time you are the path and you are fate-
You, little, feeble sheep,
Have more power than you dare to dream."
And with that knowledge given to me by fate herself not long ago,
I realize the places she would have me tread are in fact the places I
Must go-
Not because she would have it so
But because I would have it so...
Even when I am weary and yearn for sleep
I know deep inside in that place I can not yet see-
Where I am connected to fate... this is where I must be
Because it was already so written
By me.

Conquering Fear

When the beat drops
It's like thunder landing on the table
My irises expand at the sight of this sound
The liquid bass oozes into my brain
So hot its lava leaves flames in its path
The world around me is deaf to the boom
While my eardrums crack
From the sound of liberation
I walk to the beat of this drum
Sometimes that means sacrifice and complication
Sometimes that means I crack the ground I stand on
Revealing my depth
To the deaf world

## My Song

I wandered into the shadow of death
Deep inside the earth
Where the sun did not tread
Silence surrounded me
Immobilized with fear I waited
I waited for guidance
I waited for direction
Time passed
And passed
And passed
Until it ceased to exist
I began to wonder
If I'd been there forever
I'd forgotten how to see
And how to speak
Then I heard a song
Faint as a newborn's breath
So I stirred
Turning my head to catch its direction
And hope melted into me
Slow flowing like honey
Filling up my toes
And into my ankles
As the song grew
As sweet as the molasses
Engulfing me
I felt my mass again
My place in this world
So I let this song guide me
Through the shadow of death
And when I finally emerged
I found this song
Was mine all along

*Liya Endale*

We are Eternal

We are anchored to this body like gravity anchors this body to Earth. We try to make sense of this space around us like fish in a bowl. This space not separated from time. We are wedged in this gridlock somewhere between tomorrow and the sun. When we return to our elements, we turn into everything, everywhere. That is our essence even now. We are eternity.

*Contradictions: Self Empowerment*

Change

The world takes a leap forward
We stagger
Catch our balance
And adapt
Accept change
Like the Earth
Around a volcano
Rewritten with
Each eruption
The world shifts
And we go with it

*Liya Endale*

Conquering Demons

You violated me
With one touch
We birthed a demon
Who made noise in my head
Ceaseless noise
I tried to escape
Regardless of where I ran
He was there waiting
Until his noise became normal
I learned to think through it
I learned to live and love despite of it
And one day, I learned to forgive
And each day since then
This demon dies a little until
There is silence
In that part of me

Transcending Judgment

As a young girl, I tried to make sense of it all, wading through waters well above my head. I had not yet learned to swim. An extremist, I had to fit things into boxes. Black goes here. White goes there. There is no room for gray. I had to know how someone who everyone, even myself, thought was so good could do something so bad. For years I decided that his good was an illusion. It was not real. So I judged him by his one bad act. Then, as I got older, I began to see how easy it was to contradict our own set of morals and values. We disappoint ourselves with decisions we make that we do not understand. Then, it is easy to capitulate and say, I am a bad person. The good I've done is an illusion. This is who I really am. That is when I learned that good people do bad things. However, bad people do good things, too.

Now, I think past boxes. Black goes here. White goes there. Good goes there. Bad goes here.

I once heard an old Native American tale. It told of two wolves that battle in each of us. One is good and one is evil. As a grandmother explained this concept to her grandchild, the grandchild grew worried and asked, "Which wolf will win?"
The grandmother replied, "The one you feed."

**LIKE THE RAIN IN PARIS**

**(A SHORT STORY)**

Mignolita

When the rain falls in Paris, everything about it is different. It smells different. It feels different. It sounds different. The drops of water do not fall out of the sky and splash to the Earth. They seem to step down from the clouds and disappear among us as though they have a place here. I look through the haze at the French people passing by; some in a hurry and others not seeming to notice the rain that has soaked their clothes which now cling to their bodies. Under the protection of the taffy colored awning of a coffee shop, I lift the delicate violin to my chin and begin playing solos from Aram Khachaturian's Violin Concerto in D Minor. To me, this arrangement sounds like rain in all its form; frantic scurry to peaceful nostalgia. Improvising where my imaginary symphonic accompaniment falls on deaf ears, I close my eyes and get lost in the sound. I give up control of my fingers to the instrument and they slide up and down her neck. The bow sometimes crunches with friction and, other times, glides along her strings like soft butter. After my 12 and a half minute rendition I slowly open my eyes to watch the last note disappear into the crowd like the rain. I've caught a few spectators, mostly customers of the shop who nod and smile in approval as they sip their steaming lattes. I thank the little girl who coyly places a silver and copper Euro in the burgundy velvet of my case and scurries back to her mother's side.

"Merci, Ma petite," and she blushes madly.

This is how I have spent my days since I boarded a plane three years ago from the U.S., where I am from, to London. In the 6th grade a young Italian violinist happened to land in my hometown to follow some romantic notion in the shape of a blonde haired, green eyed woman. Other than his music, she was the only love in his life. For some reason, he, Antonio Alessandri, saw some potential in me- a bony, frizzy haired girl with small hands and strong fingers. I was an awkward loner on the fringes of middle school society- perhaps partly because I could not understand the use for a training bra or a boy (or they could not understand the use for me). So, though it got tedious at times, I became my worst critic and fingered away at the notes Antonio, Mr. Alessandri at the time, would challenge me with. They began to stretch in range and the pages of music got darker as more and more notes were squeezed into the same tick-tock of the metronome. He even began playing with me after school, entering me in every competition as far as my folks would dare to let me venture. The sound of Italian became comfortable as I inadvertently learned more words. He would be so engrossed in critiquing my every movement, translating his thoughts to English became too much of a nuisance to keep up. I quickly learned to play faster when I'd hear "Prestissimo!" and to force myself to move at a snail's pace when he'd yell "Largo, Largo!" I quickly knew to say "Mi spiace," when I knew I did not practice enough that week and needed to lighten his mood by appealing to his soft heart.

That was my introduction to the violin, a safe platform on which to grow my technique and passion for this gift. That became my identity at school, the awkward girl who was a really good violinist. I played in talent shows and even entered the high school pageant. I couldn't walk in heels or articulate a cogent response to the question about how I planned to save the world. But I did take the audience's breath away with Seitz's Concerto No. 5. I had finally mastered double stops. When I graduated, I wasn't prepared for the expectations of college. I didn't know what I wanted to do with my life. All I knew was that I wanted to play my violin all the time. My parents were not happy with this decision but patiently obliged my journey to self discovery.

I remember the day my mother recognized that I was hopelessly bored with a small town that had no place for a mulatto girl in love with her violin. Her dark, flawless skin stretched tightly over her regal cheekbones. Her eyes, wrinkled at the corners and set deep beneath her brow, looked at me differently that day. She told me things about when she met my father, who was downstairs in the office, that even he did not know. She spoke of how Dad's mother had pulled her to the side at his sister's wedding and implored her to think twice about getting serious with her son. My grandmother, whom I barely knew, told my mother that the town would talk and no one would come to their wedding or accept her children because this was a respectable town with old traditions. Because my father is White.

"She was right." My mother explained. "Your father and I sacrificed everything for love and that was enough for us. We've been selfish because we never stopped to ask if this is enough for you."

Antonio was now married with a little brown-eyed boy who spoke with a southern drawl. He still worked with me, and I even gave lessons to some of the students in his classes. Though he critiqued my playing relentlessly, I would, every once in a while, see a smile threaten the corners of his thin lips as I made the instrument dance.

"You are a cingolata, Mignolita." My nickname, Mignolita, meant little finger or pinkie. "When will you go away and become a delfina?" He was calling me a caterpillar who had not yet transformed into her full potential.

"My mother thinks I'm already a butterfly, Antonio. Besides,doesn't a caterpillar have to build a cocoon? I'm claustrophobic."

He would shake his head and mutter to himself in Italian. I later realized he could see my yearning to be somewhere that appreciated me despite my transparent attempt at hiding this unhappiness with sassy remarks.

"Besides, Antonio, how will you and I ever get married if I'm off becoming a butterfly somewhere?"

"Non esere cretino, Mignolita. I need a donna reale. You're just a child. When you are a delfina, then my wife should worry."

"I'm not being silly, Antonio. I'm being serious!" I teased him, "But in that case, your wife has nothing to worry about." Not meant as self depracating but in somber resolve, I continued, "I'll never be a real donna like her. She always smells like expensive perfume and wears panty hose. I only wear panty hose when my mom makes me go to church." I made a face at the thought of sitting in those hard, wooden seats for two hours trying not to scratch every square inch of my prickly legs.

After realizing that the money I earned from violin lessons would not even buy a new bow and bridge for my aging instrument, I decided to explore the world. My mother helped convince my father that this was, in fact, a good idea instead of a dangerous mistake. I remember getting a postcard from Paris when I was still in middle school from my father's sister, the aunt who had been married the day my grandmother laid heavy truths upon my mother. The picture was of a fountain in a cobble stoned town square. A couple sat on its concrete ledge and people were walking all around in every direction, caught in various moments. Their emotions, thoughts and burdens painted into this postcard photo. In the background was a woman, clearly not the focal point of the shot. But she was the one who captivated me. Her face was distorted and partially covered by her thick curly hair, but the eye that shown was closed. Her chin rested on a violin, its wood so dark it seemed almost black.

I didn't know anyone in Paris at the time. But my father had a cousin in London. I convinced my father to talk her into letting me stay with her for a little while. She was a young associate in a company situated in the heart of the business center. After a several conversations with her, she agreed to host me for the season. I packed my postcard and everything I loved into a duffel bag and my violin case and headed to London. She lived in a decent flat in the heart of Brixton, a Southwestern suburb of London where reggae music and the smell of raw meats from the markets permeated the streets by day. By night Brixtonites would congregate around the pubs spread intravenously within the neighborhoods. I had no idea London could be so diverse. I stayed in the living room of the two room flat. By two room, I mean a bedroom and a living room. The small kitchen/laundry room was crammed in the back of the flat next to the bathroom. The dishwasher, a luxury, was under the kitchen sink right next to the washing machine so you could wash your dishes and your underwear side by side. My room overlooked a patio with no door to get to it. I would crawl out of the window and look over the street one floor below me. I quickly found a band of musicians, a drummer, guitarist/lead singer and keyboardist who invited me to their rehearsals. They played an eclectic array from blues to jazz to classic rock. I had a blast with them and began playing at their gigs. London loved music. I soon began filling my evenings with various appointments from weddings to art exhibits and festivals and was able to save quite a bit at the end of the summer. I invested in a pick-up, a violin bridge equipped with a sensor that changed sound to electrical signals. I could now plug my violin into an amplifier and make it hiss and buzz like an electric guitar.

My dad's cousin and I didn't see much of each other as she worked by day and I by night. When my time with her ended, I realized I had saved enough money to venture about on my own. With all the courage and money I could muster, I packed up my life savings and began to travel. I followed and trusted my violin. I stayed in rooms I'd rent by the month and sometimes in hostels full of worldly travelers. I found a culture of musicians who embraced me and, one day, I realized I did not feel so awkward anymore. We were each different and sometimes didn't even speak the same language. But when we came together with our instruments and spoke in this language of music, there was no separation between us.

That first winter, the cold forced us into stuffy restaurants, lounges and clubs, but we didn't mind. It was in one of these smoky jazz lounges in London that I met the man who would be my first real love affair. A wanderer like me, he had a long pony-tail made of soft brown curls and chain smoked Winstons. I couldn't, for the life of me, figure out how he had the lung capacity to make his saxophone rip holes into air. We were both booked with our bands to play consecutively one Thursday night in December. I had to take the tube to a different district than was indicated on my pass and uncomfortably flirted with the security attendant to get by. I did not have any cash on me, and I desperately needed the gig to pay the rent for the dingy flat I was occupying. Arriving late and out of tune, my band members threw me some glares icier than the weather outside. However, as soon as I squeezed my instrument between my collar bone and my cheek, nothing else mattered. I listened to her carefully as I slowly found the precise tension for each of her strings to resonate at the right pitch. My stiff fingers needed a few quick scales to warm up, and I jumped right in as confident as I'd ever been. The blue-grassy feel of the music was easy to become lost in. Improvising in ways I never had, I caught notes in mid air that I had never noticed sneak by me before. Syncopating the rhythm allowed me to fill in all the right spaces in the song. During the violin solo, the room was completely quiet, a difficult thing to accomplish in evening pubs. I held everyone at the tip of my bow and made them wait in anticipation for each note. Finally, when I gave them what they wanted, they were up in roars as the rosin erupted from the bridge of my instrument in a cloud of dust. The black finger board glistened with sweat from my fingers underneath the spot- light and the horse hairs from my bow began to fray as they gave way to the intensity. That was my moment, the moment I transformed under the smoky lights of a London Jazz lounge and emerged a delfina. And there he was to witness the metamorphosis, a long-haired, thirty-something renegade with a charming British accent, smelling of cigarettes. When I noticed him I was full of a new found confidence that disregarded the freckles across my nose and discovered lady curves on my body I'd never known before.

## Michael

I am ashamed to call myself a musician because this is my first encounter with an electric violin. At least it seems to be an electric violin. My saxophone is resting comfortably in its stand on stage. I was attempting an intimate rendezvous with Jack Daniels and Winston Light. In my shadowy corner of the club, an interruption threatens my resolve to remain uninterested in the world. The sound of a buzzing violin forces me to lift my eyes towards the stage. First, the strangeness of this sound catches my attention, and I don't quite know what to make of it. The girl, probably in her early twenties, looks just as strange to me and has the energy of a young new musician trying to stake her claim in this harsh business. Bewildered, I sit up, leaning into the shaft of light spilling onto my table in time to catch her eye. They are a light shade of brown, like amber tree sap accentuated by the dark hue of bark beneath it. They pierce their way to the back of the room where I sit yearning for inconspicuous disregard. She is completely engrossed in the music as her afro of curls bounces up and down with the rhythm she manipulates into an off-beat jazz hybrid. She isn't especially tall or short, especially beautiful or plain. There is just a way about how she plays her violin that I find especially captivating, the way she looks at me subconsciously as she plays her instrument- feeding off the energy of a crowd that loves her. Does she realize she's staring at me? Does she even see me or is she just duplicitously fixed upon an object as she churns out an impressive array of notes? I sit back into the shadows once again as she closes her eyes, beginning a furious attack on the strings that the crowd goes mad for. Is that smoke coming from her instrument? I chuckle. This bloody girl is on fire.

*Contradictions: Like the Rain in Paris*

Mignolita

I thought Michael would be extraordinary. I fell madly in love with him within days. He was so poised and intelligent. He had seen so much of this world he had a story for every place I dreamed of, even Paris. I was so in love with him that it did not bother me that when I would kiss his soft, stained lips, he tasted of stale cigarettes. I even learned to love it. He looked at me like no one had. It was as though he saw the real me and loved it. There was nothing I had to be embarrassed or ashamed about.

The more time we spent together, the less I played my violin. We went around town watching movies and eating exotic dishes he introduced me to. Sushi absolutely amazed me with its erotic texture and ability to satiate a latent carnal desire I did not know I had. For his birthday in February, I played him a private concert of music that reminded me of him and songs that I had written while inspired by him. He even smiled as he held me the entire night. By April, I started to suspect that he was losing interest in us. He began to criticize. Why didn't I play my violin anymore? Why did we spend so much time together? He said I didn't give him room to pursue his music and that spending time with me kept him from booking the gigs he needed. I felt humiliated. I had mistaken his gazes and tender touch for reciprocal emotions. I thought he was as enthralled in me, in us, as I was. I realized that love was not new for him. He had been here before. And there was something about this place that did not suit him.

Resolved not to torture myself with a complicated break-up, I told him I was leaving the same day I boarded an overnight ferry to Amsterdam. I was determined not to let the tears fall until my back was turned. And fall they did as though they had a place here in the midst of my heartache, like the rain in Paris.

Michael

    I am ashamed to say I feel relief when she tells me she's leaving. If only it were because the things I told her were true. Guilt is something I've learned to live with and I carry it well. Holding her in my arms has brought me alive in ways I never thought possible and, frankly, that scares the bloody hell out of me. Not even a tear as we kiss goodbye at the dock. Nor does she turn back once for a last look. This girl is stronger than I gave her credit for. The sting of regret hovers over. But I stand silently, reaching in my knickers pocket for a lighter drawn to the fag waiting behind my ear. Realizations wash over me. She's not a coward like me. I was lucky to have had her and I'm glad she's gone because I don't deserve her. Another goodbye.

## Mignolita

Amsterdam was dense, full of determined people who always had something to do. The history gave the streets a flavor that tasted of somber wisdom. The Red Light District held a truth easily avoided by families who did not cross the block to that side. It was more challenging to maneuver about because I did not speak Dutch. A chipper language that had a lot of throaty sounds and, to me, was indistinguishable from German at first. I slowly realized that the difference between the two had more to do with tone than words. Many people who spoke Dutch had something of a sing-song quality to their words that made you believe they were always happy to see you when they greeted you. Often, when someone spoke German, their words would end on a lower pitch, making them sound more serious. It was all beautiful like music.

Quickly, I learned to move out of the way when I heard the "Tring-Tring" of a speeding bicycle. I once saw an couple cycling side by side. They must have been in there sixties. The man's arm was draped over the shoulder of his lover as though they were strolling in the park. I stayed in the streets all day long, making my instrument whine, hiss and echo along with all kinds of musicians in the squares. And when there were none who wanted to play, I'd resort to the chiming sounds of Bach, Vivaldi, and Mozart that everyone seemed to enjoy. I played Vivaldi's Seasons, especially Autumn, because these songs were my home. The patterns they required of my fingers were so familiar they created a surreal world able to transform the strangest place into a safe haven. There, I could rest my head, if even for a moment.

Floating idly on small boats, we played lazy songs to the lethargic canals in the spring. We ventured to small, cobble stoned villages, getting giddy from the array of beers the people so proudly brewed. I met my best friends who would change faces in each town I happened into. I got close to no one, but connected with everyone. In the summer, we ventured off to the tulip gardens that helped dull the ache in my chest, and in the middle of a field splashed with reds, yellows, violets and whites as far as I could see, I vowed to my instrument never again to neglect her for someone who could break my heart.

By the end of Summer, I was getting anxious to leave that place. A touring band took me in. Their manager anxiously had me sign a brief contract when he heard me play one night. He was a short, stout Frenchman named Jacques, looking as mean as his smoker's cough sounded. Weary of the way he always cleared his throat before he spoke, I wondered if I had made a mistake when I agreed to finish their tour with them. Signing the contract, however, meant a steady paycheck and a place to sleep for 6 months. So, we played in Belgium, whizzed through Italy and made our way to Berlin, Germany. In Berlin, the band had a deal to play at local venues for the remainder of the 3 months I would be on contract with them. The venues were amazing; I'm talking real classy red velvet cushions, top shelf liquor, and our own dressing room. Jacques subtly hinted that I should purchase some attire that did not consist of cargo pants and spaghetti strap tank tops. The hair dresser even flat ironed my hair straight sometimes and would comb it down in a swoop across my face and tuck it behind my ear. Not recognizing myself, I marveled at its silky reach half-way down my back. It was this stranger reflected in the mirror who reminded me that time was not waiting for me. Things were changing. I had not seen my parents in a year and a half and I briefly pondered their reaction to who their little girl had become. My new manager often scolded me for not honing my musical career.

"You can be rich already. You come with me to Paris. I make you rich. You are silly girl. Why you don't make more money? You sound a beautiful on violin, like a...eh... how you say papillon?"

"Butterfly, Jacques. That's how you say papillon in English."

That day, I made another vow. This time, I told the stranger in the mirror that I would no longer allow the music I made to be forgotten as soon as it escaped the memory of all who heard it. Jacques told me if I followed him to Paris he would make me rich. Enough people had broken their promises for me to take this man sporting a funny mustache with a grain of salt. But I knew this may be my only chance to see the city of my dreams. So I would go.

In the meantime, I indulged in all that Berlin had to offer. I spend hours walking along the remnants of the Berlin wall that had transformed into a mural of expression stretching for miles. Each section of the dilapidated concrete held someone's perspective of the history of this troubled city, some painful and deep, others hopeful and optimistic. The former site of the gateway between East and West Germany became a stage of expression for artists of all sorts. People eerily painted as statues would stand still and frighten unsuspecting tourists walking by. Mimes shouted all kinds of sad stories in a universal language of motion. And music, oh the music! It filled the air and would lure me closer with its fingers of sound.

The city reminded me of Atlanta. It was absolutely enormous. I would call a hostel desk random nights of the week and ask where there was a reggae club or a jazz lounge open. Without fail, there was a response every time. The people were rugged and had experienced the good and the bad of life. This made them beautiful. And when I grew tired of the never ending array of activities to involve myself in, I would write. I wrote down the songs that had haunted my dreams and played in my imagination as the soundtrack of my life. I wrote songs to tell people the joy and the pain, the anger and the gratitude I felt. And when I introduced these songs to my violin, she seemed to understand the place from which they were born and sang them honestly. By the end of four months in Berlin, I was anxious to do something with the compilation I had put together. Jacques had tears in his eyes when I shared the music with him and they actually tumbled down his cheek when I told him I would go to Paris so he could help me record my first album.

"But I need to find a drummer, a pianist, and a guitarist to play the parts I wrote for those instruments."

"Oui, visibliment! Fille cucul..." He laughed as he wrapped his burly arms around me in a bear-hug.

When our tour bus crossed over into France, my heart began to beat harder. When we approached the outskirts of Paris, I could hardly breathe. I had waited so long for this day, I couldn't believe I was living it. The open stretches of farm land had become more and more dense until we found ourselves on city streets. The sun sat high in a blue sky. Our bus came to a stop on the curb in front of a hotel tucked between a restaurant and a market. I stepped out onto the sidewalk and looked around in wonder at the people, the buildings and the trees. "It's so nice to finally meet you." I thought to myself and then welcomed the big grin that took over my face. Jaque chuckled heftily. I threw my things in my room and grabbed my violin. I was back outside within the hour, walking and playing and talking to people who couldn't understand me. We just smiled and laughed a lot. And then I noticed something about the ground beneath my feet. The concrete changed to little rounded stones and the street opened up into a large open space with a fountain in the middle. It had a concrete ledge. The naked woman and her child stood gazing at each other the same way as in their postcard picture. My breath was caught in my throat. When I convinced myself I wasn't dreaming, I frantically reached into my case and pulled out the weathered postcard. Holding it up, I realized I could have been standing in the same place as the photographer. His name was Edgar McClarin. It said so on the back in very small print. Holding up the postcard, I realized my hand was shaking. I clutched it close to my chest and sat on the cobble stones beneath my feet. Like a volcano, I felt the emotion stir in my belly and slowly erupt up through my heart and chest and explode into clear liquid that spewed from my eyes. I had not cried in years, and I could not articulate what had caused this strange and embarrassing explosion, but I did not try to stop it. It somehow felt good, as though I was releasing so much tension stemming from heartbreak, self-doubt, insecurity and loneliness. It was as though I had been looking for something without realizing it, for my whole life. And now, I had found it. My place in this world.

 I had to give it to Jacques. He didn't make me rich, but he did everything else he promised, even helping me to find musicians. The really good ones were a bit dodgy, so I decided to go with the ones who were just beginning, like I was two short years earlier. Recording was actually the easy part. Jacques had a small studio outside of Paris that did not have a lot of equipment or space. Certainly, it was perfect for my project. In eight months the album was recorded, taking two months to find and teach their parts to the musicians. Then, we spent two weeks per song in the studio and finally had the album mastered professionally.

As I waited for the final product, I began to plan my CD release party. By then, a year of playing in Paris professionally had given me quite a reputation with local business owners. I chose a coffee house on the corner of the main square where my statue stood. All of the shops bustled with gorgeous young people pierced in odd places, sporting styles that had not yet made their way abroad. The owner was an olive skinned lady in her forties with an attitude to make up for what she lacked in height. She liked me. I didn't drink too much and kept my promises to her when she would let me play in her shop at night, Café le Amore. As my music became more popular, it also brought business to her as well.

I made hundreds of fliers and hired the local street kids to help me disseminate them for a great price. They were very efficient, too.

"Aboutir Café'de Amor!" the gang would shout, getting everyone's attention about the last opportunity to see Paris' own Violin Girl who uses the voice of her violin to sing the songs of her heart.

The night of the party, I slipped into a yellow silk dress with satin sandals and a pearl necklace. My hair was professionally curled and pulled into a loose bun behind my ear. I helped the olive skinned lady decorate the place with string lights. People began to trickle in at first, but sooner than I'd imagined the room filled up and the crowd spilled outside to the patio. Making my rounds, I thanked all of the familiar faces- people I had played with over the years and people who had received my music well. On stage, my violin sat patiently, freshly polished and tuned. The microphone was turned on and awaited my christening. The first time I spoke in front of a crowd with my own voice.

"Thank you all for coming. You look amazing from up here." The feedback squealed from one of the ground speakers and I took a step back, laughing nervously.

"Please forgive me for speaking English. I'm afraid you wouldn't get much out of a speech in French because my French is already bad, but it's terrible when I'm nervous," a few claps of encouragement gave me courage. "I suppose I wanted to actually explain to you why I do what I do. You see, I'm madly in love. There is only one who understands me without words, who knows a song to sing for every one of my emotions, who is like me- delicate and deceptively fragile by appearance, but really so strong. You'd never know it unless you took the time to know us. When I haven't felt my love's neck beneath my fingertips, it's as though I become lost and don't know who I am anymore. And tonight, we want to share this love and songs of strength with you. So without further ado, I'd like you all to meet the love of my life." Pulling out my violin I signaled the band to start the first song. I took the crowd on a journey with me, through all of the places that I had been, conveying my every emotion and re-discovering my every adventure. I laid myself out on that stage and gave them every part of me.

*Contradictions: Like the Rain in Paris*

Antonio

When my wife left me after fifteen years, my world stopped. Everything I was and everything I had known no longer is. My son left with her, now without a father. This is not what I imagined my life to be. I called the only one I had left, my own little brother who lives in Paris now. I slept on his couch for days at a time, unable to face the next moment without numbing the throb of my spirit with vodka. A month later I run out of my clear liquid potion and my brother refuses to bring me more. Furious at his callous disregard to my damaged heart I pry myself from the couch to go to the liquor store myself. Imagine my surprise when a small boy about my son's age thrusts one of about a hundred fliers he's holding into my gut and exclaims,

"Don't miss Paris's very own Violin Girl! It's your last chance to listen to her play her instrument here, she can play anything!"

"What do you know about a violin! Get this nonsense out of here." I snarl.

"You'd be stupid not to go, old man! It's your own loss," and he moves on through the crowd, unfazed.

Tearing the paper in half I happen to glance at the picture on the flier. The world starts spinning around me. It is my very own Mignolita. I barely recognize her with her hair streaming down over her shoulder and her figure accentuated by the dress she wears. But there is that same awkward way she held the bow that I could never break her out of- index finger stretched out away from the others. Unbelievable. The show is tonight, a CD release party. It is the first time I have smiled in months.

The water from the shower feels as though it penetrates my very soul. The razor on my face seems to shave away layers of self-pity I am drowning in. Did it just get a little easier to breath? I put on a suit from my brother's closet and polish my shoes. I can not have my Mignolita seeing me in the state I am in.

She makes my heart stop beating for fear of missing the next note. The crowd seems to hold its breath as she tells them a story without words. I always knew there was something inside of that girl. It shown through her eyes from the first day I met her.

"Let me see your hands, child." I had instructed the scared little girl who walked into my classroom so long ago. "Your fingers are small but they are strong, Mignolita."

"That's not my name, sir." She stammered.

"What, Little Finger? Why, of course it is, Mignolita. I've got the perfect instrument for you. Now, hold her up to your chin like this. Let's see if you can figure out how to make her sing for you."

I follow this journey Mignolita tells the crowd from the very beginning because I was there when the real journey started. After the performance it takes nearly an hour to get close enough to her for her to hear me. With vodka in my hand I squeeze through the crowd behind her.

"Hello, delfina." She freezes for a moment and turns around slowly, her eyes wide with disbelief.

"Is it really... you?"

"You still need to fix your position. I told you about your grip on the bow. But you were always stubborn."

"Antonio! I can't believe this! How did you... where have you..." Her eyes well up, the first time I had seen this hard girl cry, and she embraces me burying her face into my neck. I put my arms around her, using all my energy not to become too emotional. That night we talk for hours, long after the crowd has left and the fiery little Italian owner closes the doors. I tell her about my wife. She tells me about her adventures. She says she is so sorry for what I am going through and we cry together until we feel silly for it. I tell her I am proud of her and she says that means everything coming from me. I can't hide that I was a broken man and with my Mignolita I don't need to. After a lot of drinks in our private Café le Amore, I admit to her how beautiful she has become, a donna real. She has always been so smart, that girl. And when I lean in to kiss her she stops me.

"Antonio, this is not right. You've had a lot to drink. I know you must be feeling so lost right now but I am not your answer. I'm sorry, I can't do this. I hope you understand."

Completely mortified, I am broken down to nothing .The rejection kills what little life my ego has left. I stumble out of my chair in the only emotion that is strong enough to rear its head, anger.

"No. I do not understand. Maybe you're just not the true donna you pretend to be on stage. You can put on a pretty dress and paint your face, but I know you now. You almost fooled me, little girl. You'll never be a donna enough for a man like me!" I don't look back to see the pain I want to inflict in her eyes.

Mignolita

His words sear me like a hot brand on cattle's skin, claiming its property.

"I caused this pain and created this scar!"

Then, I remember the magic of the night and the realizations come to me. He is a broken man. This woman stole his identity from him. If I lost my music I would be nothing, like he is now. My pain turns to pity as I watch a drunk old man stumble into the shadows of the allies in Paris.

# Antonio

I wake up feeling as though an elephant is perched on my temple. There is no energy in this old body. As I slowly recall the events of last night, I begin to hate myself again. What have I done? The last thing I want is to steal the hope and innocence of a beautiful girl. She did not deserve those things I said. What exactly did I say? I don't know. I need water. Then I will go and find her to apologize. She mentioned that she will be at the café today before she leaves.

When I step outside, I am met by the cool water raining from the sky. It feels good on my skin, like liberation. I make my way to the café where Mignolita is playing a beautiful song. Khachaturian. Her improvisations reform the piece into a harmony to this very moment, to the sound of the rain. It becomes painfully obvious. This delfina has no need for my apologies. Someone's already taken her hope and her innocence away. Her beauty is that she's regained it, all on her own. I watch a little girl throw money into the violin case and shy away. Mignolita accepts it humbly as if she had not just sold out of every single copy she had of her new album last night at her cd release party. I can tell she's thinking of me as she wipes the rosin from her bow, looks at her index finger extended awkwardly up the shaft of the wood and smiles to herself. I do not approach her as she hauls the case onto her back. There is nothing I can do but taint this perfect moment so I choose to observe it from afar, instead. And as she walks away from me with a bag in her hand, she seems to disappear into the crowd like the rain in Paris.

# ABOUT THE AUTHOR

Liya Endale is an Ethiopian born U.S. citizen who left her birth-land due to political strife. As an asylum seeker in The Netherlands for five years, she and her family learned to speak Dutch and got accustomed to snowy winters and beautiful summers. Her journey would then take her to Texas and, finally, Atlanta, Georgia, where she now resides with her husband and son. After receiving her M.Ed in school counseling, Liya started the non-profit, Global Education Foundation, Inc. With the ambition of making education available for everyone everywhere, she is offering her motivational speaking, spoken-word workshops and books available as tools to facilitate accessible education.

For booking information: www.globaleducationfoundationinc.org.

www.ingramcontent.com/pod-product-compliance
Lightning Source LLC
Chambersburg PA
CBHW031202090426
42736CB00009B/762